FIRENZE
MVSEI

Museum
of the Opificio
delle Pietre Dure

ANNAMARIA GIUSTI

sillabe

Firenze Musei
is a registered
trademark of
Sergio Bianco

FIRENZE
MVSEI

ISBN 978-88-8347-282-4
© 2007 Ministero per i Beni e le Attività Culturali
Opificio delle Pietre Dure

A publication by
s i l l a b e s.r.l.
Livorno
www.sillabe.it
info@sillabe.it

The diagrams of the Museum's rooms
have been kindly provided by Giovanni Breschi.

managing editor: *Maddalena Paola Winspeare*
graphic design: *Laura Belforte*
editing: *Giulia Bastianelli*
translation: *Catherine Burnett*

series design: *Franco Bulletti*
photolithography: *La Nuova Lito-Firenze*

photographs: *Archivio Sillabe/Foto Paolo Nannoni;
Archivio Fotografico SSPMF Firenze*

Contents

This new guide book for the Museum of the Opificio delle Pietre Dure, like the previous version published in 1995, was overseen by the director Annamaria Giusti. It is an updated and comprehensive book which allows us to fully appreciate the collections and their organisation in the historical location of 78 Via degli Alfani.

In recent years interest in applied arts and its splendid handcrafted objects (like the stone 'commesso' or Florentine mosaics, marquetry and 'scagliola") has grown on a national and international level. This is partly due to the research, restoration and cultural awareness activities carried out by experts like Annamaria Giusti. Thanks to the substantial experience of the stone "commesso" and mosaic restoration department, directed by Annamaria Giusti, many extremely important works of art in semi-precious stones have been sent to the Opificio for specialist conservation procedures; the works include *Queen Margaret's Chest of Drawers* and the *Table Top with Tulips*. Furthermore thanks to the Opificio's acknowledged specialist status, it has been invited to oversee the technical aspects of the *Art of the Royal Court: Treasures in Pietre Dure from the Palaces in Europe* exhibition due to take place at the Metropolitan Museum in New York in 2008.

The semi-precious stone 'commesso' was costly and valued which made it a courtly art par excellence. A rich variety of 'commessi' can be seen at the Museum of the Opificio and they never fail to stimulate visitors whether they are students enraptured by the wonderful materials, or enthusiasts of different origin and educational background fascinated by the technical expertise of the craftsmen. The production of the old Galleria dei Lavori makes up a central part of this Museum. The displays evoke the magnificence of the Tuscan dynasties before Italy became unified to the highest degree: the Medici family's three-century reign was especially significant, then came the Hapsburg-Lorraine and Savoy dynasties. All these families are linked, from an objective point of view, by a common plus point: they all left the Opificio as a 'free' State workshop, allowing it to work without interruption but also accepting and guiding it through change in order to convey its legacy of antique knowledge unharmed into future.

The Museum of the Opificio is also one of the few Florentine museums to have had a complete renovation. In 1995 a new layout was inaugurated after four years of work; the work was overseen by Annamaria Giusti when Giorgio Buonsanti was the Opificio's director. The re-organization, planned by Adolfo Natalini and directed by Marco Magni, created a well structured and varied display area within the limits of the space available. The display area's subsections along the length of the gallery were split onto two levels thanks to the introduction of a mezzanine; this space is dedicated to materials, tools and techniques. The Opificio's simple structural design and elegant furnishings make it an impeccable model; it is a place full of wonderful objects worthy of a *Wunderkammer* which presents its displays with such lucid organisational clarity, it almost resembles an encyclopaedia.

The Museum's renovation has not only attracted compliments; important donations have been made to the collections including a series of punches belonging to the Siries dynasty of artistic directors (recently displayed in the exhibition *Arte e Manifattura di Corte a Firenze*, held at the Palazzo Pitti in 2006) and a photo album from the Holy Land which has a semi-precious stone 'commesso' plaque on the cover showing the Savoy family coat of arms. These donations are also a tangible sign of the vitality of the Museum and the Institute it is a part of. The Opificio's work over more than four centuries certainly doesn't seem to have weighed it down.

Cristina Acidini
Superintendent of the Polo Museale Fiorentino
and, *ad interim*, of the Opificio delle Pietre Dure

Not just the David!
A room full of wonders
for the curious visitor

The visitors who find their way through the never ending queues of tourists waiting to see Michelangelo's *David* and manage to enter the Museum of the Opificio at 78 Via degli Alfani will find themselves watched over kindly from above by the marble bust of Ferdinando I de' Medici, who "gave the Opificio a stable state of order" ("all'Opificio diede stabile ordina-mento") according to the 19th-century plaque underneath. As a matter of fact the Opificio of today, which is not only a museum but also a polyhedral institution dedicated to the restoration of works of art, has an ancient history which spans more than four centuries. It all started in 1588 when Ferdinando founded a Workshop destined to last through the ages.

Ferdinando I, the second son of Cosimo I de' Medici, was a great patron of the arts and a wise governor. He gave the artistic workshops lodged in the Uffizi a rigorous organisational structure and a united face as from then on they were known as the 'Galleria dei Lavori', working exclusively for the Medici court. The speciality and pride of the grand-ducal workshops soon became the crafting of semi-precious stones; the technique reached such unequalled levels of excellence that the reigning Medici passed on their passion for the sparkling polychrome stones to all their descendants like a hereditary gene. They also used them to attract attention and admiration for their flourishing court Workshop from all over Europe. After the Renaissance Florence had lost its leading role in the field of 'arti maggiori' (major guilds) but during the 17th and 18th centuries it entrusted its international prestige to the imaginative creativity and staggering technique of the semi-precious stone work.

The 'Florentine mosaic' figures prominently in the stone workmanship, the finished image is an ingenious, magically unified puzzle which originates from countless pieces of semi-precious stones. The stones are shaped and cut with painstaking precision in order to guarantee a perfect fit between the different parts then set together according to structurally complex outlines. The definition 'paintings of stone', which is said to have been used by Grand Duke Ferdinando himself, is certainly well suited to these sophisticated mosaics, capable of handling all genres of painting from portraits to landscapes, from still life to historical compositions all with seeming ease and ductility. In reality these 'paintings of stone' are the fruit of a hard working, diligent and able technician whose aim is to amaze and seduce the observer.

However, this fascinating stone mosaic genre was not invented by the Medici of Florence, it is actually much older. Like many forms of expression of our artistic tradition, the technique originates in the civilisation of ancient Rome. It was then, from the imperial period onwards, that different types of coloured marble from various territories of the empire were amassed in Rome. It was used to make inlays to decorate pavements and walls with themes and figures. The passion for the old ways and their imitation brought the Renaissance movement towards the rediscovery of this artistic genre, which emerged in 16th-century Rome. It culminated in the era of Florentine Mannerism providing an ideal backdrop to celebrate the happy union between art and nature.

The 'beautiful stones' were by themselves worth so much money that they were an ideal object of worship for the 16th century: they excited naturalistic-scientific interest as well as inspiring magical and alchemic beliefs about their properties; from that moment onwards the stones' enchanting shades of colour and the unchanging splendour that they acquired dur-

II/13

ing the manufacturing process, successfully established an irresistible allure for both the makers' creative flair and the buyers' and collectors' enjoyment. The first Florentine mosaics were born from ingenious artifice in order to satisfy the Baroque penchant for objects and forms of expression which excited 'wondrous admiration'. This was, of course, innate in a form of artistic expression which combined luxurious materials and visual illusion: colours which seemed carefully controlled with a brush were actually the fruit of nature's fantasy; supple drawing and soft shapes were actually obtained by the makers' arduous care with the hard material; picturesque images which seemed to spring from the artist's imagination were in fact skilfully constructed by the careful and difficult juxtaposition of hundreds of pieces of stone.

Certa fulgent sidera (as sure as the shining stars) was Cosimo III de' Medici's trusted motto which, contrary to its positive meaning, saw the Tuscan Grand Duchy's decline and the Medici dynasty's imminent extinction. Although the stars didn't shine kindly on him at least the semiprecious stones were resplendent during his long reign, becoming one of the leading episodes in the history of decorative arts in Europe. The extent of their importance was illustrated when the Medici dynasty died out in 1737. The Hapsburg Lorraine suc-

II/15

ceeded to the Grand Duchy of Tuscany replacing the lavish generosity of the Medici regime with a more economic approach. However, they continued to nurture the glorious Workshop as a precious feather in their cap, furnishing the Royal Palaces in Vienna and Florence with constantly updated semi-precious stone creations. Even the members of Napoleon's family, in government for a short lived period, didn't fail to appreciate and support the production of the court Workshop. It continued, when the Lorraine dynasty returned, to have a important role in the Grand Duchy until the united Kingdom of Italy was formed in 1861.

It was the changing socio-political situation linked to this transformation which decided the future of the old Medici artistic workshops. When they were left without a local court to act as patrons and buyers, they could no longer guarantee the prosperity of such an elite and costly art. On the other hand in the second half of the 19th century the Florentine mosaic work enjoyed fame amongst a different clientele, the foreign visitors passing through Florence and, to a lesser extent, the new national bourgeois society. However, the Opificio couldn't compete against the numerous private workshops which also produced the mosaics. It proudly maintained a high quality of inventiveness and a finesse of execution which transformed its creations into expensive works of art and distanced them from the

pleasing handicraft objects produced by the other workshops. In the end, rather than betray its past, the Opificio chose a new activity and a new future that even now, over a century later, makes it precious and vital in the field of restoration: preserving and restoring works of art from Italian heritage.

The Opificio Museum invites you to discover this unique and evocative story starting with Cosimo I de Medici's passion for noble porphyry and imperial marbles from ancient Rome and culminating with the unsold and exquisite creations from the King Umberto period. Of course many beautiful items (or indeed spectacular items) created at the Opificio left the Workshop, destined for illustrious Italian or European venues. It is not therefore in our Museum, although directly linked to the workshops, that we can find the best of centuries' worth of inexhaustible creativity: the architecturally monumental cabinets with mosaics, *glyptics* (a type of sculpting often used for cameos) and jewels glittering in the brilliant ebony; the tables covered in ornamentation as a result of the creators' diligence and teamwork; the furniture, sacred and profane, where gilded silver and bronze submit to the glory of the iridescent stones; the pure rock crystals, transformed from their hard, uncut state to become perfectly transparent vases, light and iridescent like soap bubbles.

It is for this reason that we recommend to followers of the genre, or simply to those who

VI/9

love beauty, to go to the Palazzo Pitti, which was the Royal Palace of Florence and the principal collector of these works, or to the Cappella dei Principi (The Chapel of the Princes), the mausoleum of the Grand Dukes which displays their everlasting memory with the constant splendour of the semi-precious stone decorations. Superb examples of Florentine mosaics can also be seen in many Italian and European museums, from the Louvre to the Victoria and Albert, from the Grünes Gewölbe in Dresden to the Hermitage in St. Petersburg. More often than not, these pieces didn't arrive at their foreign destinations as a result of plundering or alienation but as gifts to demonstrate the

work of the small, but artistically great Grand Duchy of Tuscany.

The Museum of the Opificio came into existence when artistic activity declined at the end of the 19th century. It gathered together everything in the workshops which had been left without a destination or returned due to variations of taste and style. These works only make up a small part of the glorious Workshop's prolific production but there is, without doubt, enough material of undeniable charm to be able to tell the full story of this little known yet captivating chapter in Florentine art history.

The Museum was renovated in 1995 by Adolfo Natalini and the collection was rearranged, under my guidance, into eight

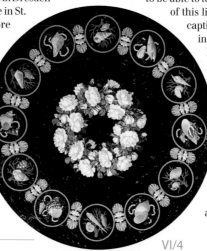

VI/4

themed sections which focus on features and styles of the work over three centuries. Thanks to its intrinsic link to the Workshop, visitors have the unique opportunity to see how these works arduously reached perfection and also to catch a glimpse of life in the workrooms. On the mezzanine level of the hall in the section entitled *Il laboratorio delle pietre dure* the display has over 600 examples of the stones which helped to create the visually stunning natural palette of the Florentine mosaics; the 18th-century work benches which are a rare testimony of the avant-garde era's technical knowledge; the stages of production from uncut 'pebbles' of silica stone to resplendent mosaics or pieces in relief; and moreover the memories and curiosities of a workshop which pursued its artistic purpose with thorough, methodical organisation.

The semi-precious stone work was not a widely known art and the quiet Opificio Museum is not designed for the mass tourism which besieges Florence today. However, those who enter will find themselves momentarily spellbound, happy prisoners of a 'room full of wonders' which not only reveals fascinating and unusual objects but also brings you closer to a world that methodically and diligently created beauty.

The visit

The works are quoted according to their number on the information panels in the rooms and in this book

(*) See in depth explanations in *The masterpieces* section

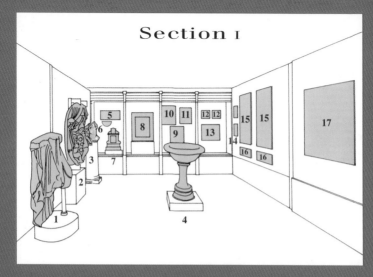

THE FIRST GRAND DUKES AND SEMI-PRECIOUS STONES

The artistic Workshop dedicated to semi-precious stone work was officially founded in 1588 by the Grand Duke Ferdinando I, but the family passion for these precious materials can be traced back to the previous century and the collections of Lorenzo the Magnificent. Cosimo, the first Grand Duke of Tuscany, shared the 16th-century enthusiasm for polychrome marble which had been decoratively used in imperial Rome. He favoured the Egyptian red porphyry as it was a traditional symbol of royal dignity and was a very fitting way to celebrate his new sovereignty. His son Francesco preferred the visually stunning palette of the semi-precious stones, worked on by masterly craftsmen both with the 'intaglio' method (a carving technique) and the mosaic technique. The stones were conveyed from Milan in order to create iridescent rock crystal vases and sophisticated marquetry (inlay work) under the fascinated gaze of the Prince. Thus the foundations were laid for an artistic tradition of excellence which made the prestigious Workshop founded by Ferdinando I famous in Europe for three centuries; it was specialised in creating polychrome stone mosaics capable of competing with paintings for creativity of composition and chromatic brilliance.

1. Roman art, *Fragment of a figure (Dacian prisoner)*, II cent. A.D., ancient red porphyry

2. Francesco Ferrucci del Tadda (attrib.), *Unfinished Medici coat of arms*, before 1585, antique red porphyry

Antique red porphyry was a symbol of imperial power and Cosimo I de' Medici's favourite material.

3. Romolo Ferrucci (attrib.), *Giant's head known as 'Alessandro dying'*, 1580–1590, antique red porphyry and white marble, formerly in the Villa Medici in Rome (fig. p. 18)

The Ferrucci Workshop specialised in the difficult porphyry work.

4. Roman art, *Basin*, antique green marble; 18th-cent. African marble stem and pink granite base

5. *'Tiretto'* (handle), 1994, semi-precious stone mosaic, gilded bronze and wood, copy made by the Opificio, from the 15th-cent. original in the Mineralogy Museum in Florence

6. Milanese or Florentine manufacture, *Goblet*, 16th cent., intaglio in rock crystal (fig. p. 19)

7. Florentine manufacture, *Shrine* (the central piece is missing), early 17th cent., ebony and semi-precious stones

8. Francesco Ferrucci, *Portrait of Cosimo I de' Medici*, 1598 (* p. 54)

9. Domenico Cresti known as il Passignano, *Cosimo I de' Medici*, 1597, oil on canvas

This was done as a design for the stone mosaic portrait (no. 8).

10. Santi di Tito, *Henry IV of France*, 1600, oil on canvas

Design for a lost stone mosaic portrait, given as a gift to the King from Maria de' Medici when they got married in 1600.

11. Roman or Venetian art, *Ferdinando I de' Medici*, late 16th cent., stone and glass tile mosaic

This mosaic portrait was highly appreciated by the Medici and was displayed among the treasures of the Uffizi tribune for a long time.

12. Grand-ducal manufacture, *Two tiles with birds on fruit tree boughs*, early 17th cent., soft stone mosaic on black marble

13. Grand-ducal manufacture, *Table top with a parrot*, early 17th cent., soft stone mosaic

14. Grand-ducal manufacture, *Two tiles with a vase of flowers*, early 17th cent., soft stone mosaic on black marble

15. *Large vase of flowers*, early 17th cent. (* p. 55)

16. Grand-ducal manufacture, *Two slabs with swans and fish*, ca 1600–1625, alabaster inlay work, painted on the back of the 'lined Arno' limestone ('alberese') (fig. pp. 18–19)

Along with the panels above with the vases of flowers (cat no. 15), this work was part of the decoration of an oratory in the Villa del Poggio Imperiale.

17. *Table top with a parrot, flowers and military trophies* (* p. 56)

I/3

I/16

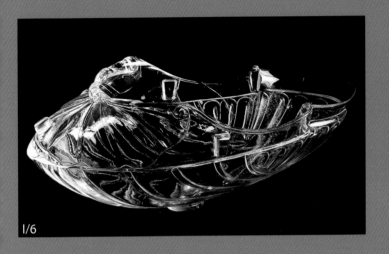

I/6

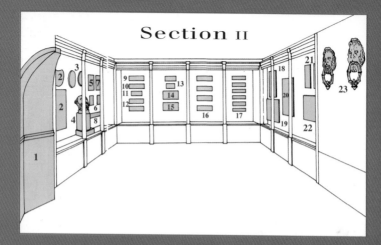

THE CAPPELLA DEI PRINCIPI

The newly founded Workshop played a lead role in Ferdinando I de' Medici's most significant architectural initiative, it was asked to use its skills for the astounding semi-precious stone decoration of the Cappella dei Principi (Chapel of the Princes) which was built in 1604. It was a superb mausoleum adjoining the Basilica of San Lorenzo for Medici family burials and, according to Ferdinando's ambitious project, was to be entirely covered in semi-precious stones from the floor to the great dome, a cupola second only to that of Brunelleschi.

The works gathered in this section demonstrate the fact that the project went on for over two centuries and experienced partial reorganisations, variations and pauses. For example the work on the radiant semi-precious stone and precious metal temple, conceived for the Chapel's central altar, began at the beginning of the 17th century but was never finished. It included landscapes and religious stories in semi-precious stones which remain among the great masterpieces of the genre, but after the 18th-century dismantlement of the altar the works were divided among various different places.

1. *Design for the Cappella dei Principi*, 1743 (* p. 57)

2. *Tuscan town coat of arms*, late 16th cent. (* p. 58)

3. Grand-ducal manufacture, *Two coats of arms*, late 16th–early 17th cent., soft stone mosaic on white marble

The coat of arms with Medici and Lorraine emblems can be traced to the wedding of Grand Duke Ferdinando and Cristina of Lorraine in 1590. The other coat of arms bears the papal insignia of Paul V (Camillo Borghese), pope from 1605 to 1621.

4. Bernardo Buontalenti and Lorenzo Latini, *Cosimo I de' Medici*, early 17th cent., red marble and stucco

Unfinished head for the funerary statue of the Grand Duke; when Buontalenti died in 1608 it was recorded as being among the works in his studio.

5. Grand-ducal manufacture, *Medici-della Rovere coat of arms*, ca 1638, semi-precious and soft stone mosaic on black marble

This coat of arms refers to the wedding of Ferdinando II de' Medici and Vittoria della Rovere

6. Girolamo Caroni, *Two panels with vases of flowers*, 1615, semi-precious stone mosaic on 'paonazzetto marble from Flanders' (rock made of fragments of white marble and purple coloured cement)

These panels can be seen in a 17th-cent. project for the altar of the unfinished Cappella dei Principi.

7. *Medici coat of arms*, 17th cent., semi-precious stone mosaic on a black background

This work is unfinished, it may have been destined for the altar in the Cappella dei Principi.

8. *Ornamental frame*, early 17th cent., lapis lazuli, Sicilian jasper and Bohemian jasper coverings for the altar in the Cappella dei Principi

9. Gualtieri Cecchi, *Samson slaying the lion*, after a drawing by Emanuele Tedesco, 1612, semi-precious stone mosaic

One of the little biblical stories destined for the altar in the Cappella dei Principi. The otherwise unheard of creator of the design was among the north European artists who came to Ferdinando I de' Medici's court.

10. *Elijah and the angel*, 1600–1620 (* p. 59)

11. Grand-ducal manufacture, *Landscape*, early 17th cent., semi-precious stone mosaic

Other than biblical and evangelical stories, the 'paintings of stone' for the unfinished altar in the Cappella dei Principi included landscapes (see nos. 12, 13).

12. *Two Tuscan landscapes*, from designs by Bernardino Poccetti, 1605–1608 (* p. 59)

13. Grand-ducal manufacture, *Two Views of northern landscapes*, probably after a design by Emanuele Tedesco (?), ca 1620–1630, semi-precious stone mosaic (fig. p. 9)

The northern character of the two river views leads us to believe that the artist who did the design was Flemish.

14. Grand-ducal manufacture, *Melchizedek and the Temple candlestick*, 1600–1620, semi-precious stone mosaic (fig. p. 22)

15. Fabiano Tedesco, *Jonah and the whale*, after a design by Emanuele Tedesco, 1612, semi-precious stone mosaic (fig. p. 9)

In this case the creator of the mosaic was also from the circle of northern European artists at the Medici court.

16. Grand-ducal manufacture, *Series of panels with fruit and flowers*, ca 1850–1860, semi-precious stone mosaic on black Belgian marble

This and other works displayed in the sequence (nos. 17–22) are linked to an 18th-cent. project, in the last years of the Tuscan Grand Duchy, to give the Cappella dei Principi a central altar. Unfortunately this project, like its 17th-cent. counterpart, was never finished.

17. Grand-ducal manufacture, *Panels with flowers and foliage*, ca 1700–1750, semi-precious stone mosaic on black Belgian marble

In the 19th-cent. project for the Cappella dei Principi altar, these panels from the Medici era were going to be used. They were based on designs left in the Workshop.

18. Giovan Battista Giorgi, *Laurel and olive garland*, ca 1820, oil on canvas design, for the mosaic no. 20

19. *Project for the altar of the Cappella dei Principi*, 1860, watercolour on paper design

The last of the 19th-cent. projects started in the 1820s was to give the Chapel a semi-precious stone altar. The project was never carried out.

20. *Laurel and olive garland*, after a design by Giovan Battista Giorgi, semi-precious stone mosaic on porphyry, made from the design at no. 18 (fig. p. 10)

21. *Two panels with a sceptre and a flaming torch*, ca 1821, chalcedony in relief on black Belgian marble

These pieces were probably part of the new project for the altar in the Cappella dei Principi and were among the first works to be produced after the restoration of Ferdinando III of Hapsburg Lorraine to the Tuscan throne.

22. *Series of 'rosettes'*, ca 1850, semi-precious stone mosaic on Egyptian nephritis

Decorative elements for the Cappella dei Principi's 19th-cent. altar.

23. *Two sculpted lion heads*, 17th cent. (?), oriental granite

These are identical to the heads on the six sarcophagi of the Medici Grand Dukes in the Cappella dei Principi.

II/14

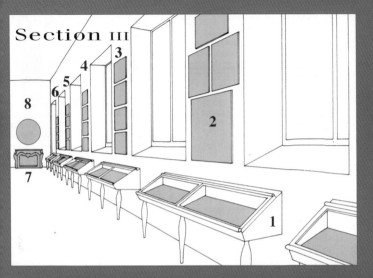

SEMI-PRECIOUS STONE FLOWERS

In the varied repertoire of subjects tackled with the semi-precious stone mosaic technique the naturalistic theme of flowers, often coupled with fruit or birds, was firmly established. It was popular throughout the 17th century and beyond, virtually becoming the 'logo' of the grand-ducal Workshop. These works gave rise to and fed the curiosity for nature which was especially great at the time of the Medici. The style combined a naturalistic interest with the passion for the beautiful polychrome stones, an especially suitable material for capturing other natural colour gradations like the changing tones of flowers and the shaded plumage of birds. The naturalistic mosaics were applied to various types of furniture from Medici workshops but it was particularly popular on cabinets and little boxes. For these popular items the craftsmen often prepared the stone panels in advance, the object could then be mounted quickly. A series of examples remains in the Museum collection.

1. Series of different panels with naturalistic subjects such as birds, flowers and fruit in various combinations, 17th and 18th cent., semi-precious and soft stone mosaics (* p. 61)

The pieces are linked by theme and destination. They were made in large quantities in the Medici Workshop in order to be ready to mount on cabinets or other similar pieces of furniture.

2. Iacopo Ligozzi, *Design for a table top with flowers*, ca 1620 (* p. 60)

3. Giuseppe Zocchi, *The four elements: Earth, Fire, Water and Air*, 1750, oil on canvas

These designs started off a series of over sixty paintings several of which are displayed in the Museum (nos. 3 and 6 in this section, and in Section v). They were prepared by Giuseppe Zocchi for semi-precious stone works

III/7

destined for the Viennese residence of Francesco Stefano of Lorraine, Grand Duke of Tuscany and Emperor of Austria. The Workshop worked almost exclusively on these designs for twenty years having passed from Medici to Lorraine control at the same time as the Grand Duchy.

4. Giuseppe Zocchi, *The four continents: Europe, Asia, Africa, America*, 1758, oil on canvas

5. Giuseppe Zocchi, *Four Views of the port of Leghorn*, 1762, oil on canvas

6. Giuseppe Zocchi, *The seasons: Autumn, Winter, Spring, Summer*, ca 1756–1757, *oil on canvas*

7. Russian manufacture, Fireplace, 19th cent., Siberian malachite and gilded bronze (fig. p. 24)

8. Giovan Battista Giorgi, *Apollo and the Muses*, 1837, oil on canvas

Design for a large circular table top in semi-precious stones, on display at the Galleria Palatina.

III/4

Europe

III/5

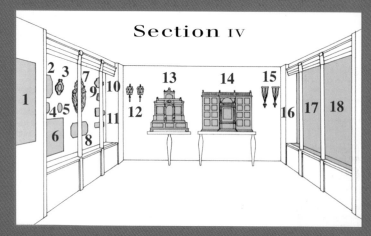

THE LAST MEDICI

The international fame which the Florentine Workshop quickly acquired led, among other things, to the creation of a counterpart semi-precious stone Workshop in Prague at the end of the 16th century. It was founded by Rudolf II of Hapsburg and employed craftsmen conveyed from Florence. Until the end of the dynasty in 1737 the Medici continued to protect and increase the output of the elaborate court Workshop. The works were often sent as gifts to sovereigns and powerful families all over Europe and became a desirable attestation of the small Tuscan court's exquisite artistic taste. The imaginative Baroque creativity was shown at its very best in the luxurious and evocative furniture; the architectural cabinets, the four-poster beds, the monumental tables and many more. All these pieces featured the semi-precious stones, often shaped with ductility, their luminosity blended with the splendour of gilded bronze.

1. Giovan Battista Foggini, *The slaying of Niobe's children*, 1674, terracotta in relief
An early work by the sculptor who was later to become director of the grand-ducal Workshop.

2. *Portrait of Ferdinando II de' Medici*, 1669, incision on rock crystal by Gerhard Walder; carved pearwood frame by Vittorio Crosten; ebony case by Leonard van der Vinne
A small but good example

of team work, in this case between international artists working for the grand-ducal Workshop.

3. *Portrait of Cosimo III de' Medici*, 1668, incision on rock crystal by Gerhard Walder; carved pearwood frame by Vittorio Crosten

4. Giuseppe Antonio Torricelli, *Cosimo III and Tuscany*, late 17th cent. (* p. 64)

5. *Portrait of the Grand Prince Ferdinando de' Medici*, ca 1680. miniature on card, in a wooden frame inlaid with ivory and tortoise shell
The frame is in the style of the great Flemish cabinet maker Leonard van der Vinne who worked for the Medici family for a long time. It encloses a portrait of Cosimo III's heir as a child. Ferdinando died before his father.

6. Orazio Mochi (sculpting) and Francesco Bianchi Bonavita (colouring), *Cosimo II de' Medici*, 1624, coloured

papier mâché in relief
Contemporary copy in inexpensive materials of the famous and precious *Ex voto of Cosimo II de' Medici,* which stands today in the Museo degli Argenti but was originally destined for the altar of the Church of San Carlo Borromeo in Milan.

7. *A bedroom holy water stoup,* early 18th cent. (* p. 65)

8. Baccio Cappelli, *Annunciation,* 1727, semi-precious stone mosaic, signed and dated on the back (fig. p. 28)

9. Cosimo Castrucci, *Fame,* after a design attributed to Bernardino Poccetti, ca 1620, semi-precious stone mosaic (fig. p. 28)
This mosaic, like no. 11, is an example of the collaboration between the Florentine Workshop and the one founded in Prague by the Emperor Rudolfo II. Designs sent from Florence were made into mosaics in Prague then sent back to the Medici court.

10. Prague manufacture, *Three landscapes,* early 17th cent., Bohemian jasper mosaic
The subject and the stones used in this work are distinctive signs of the Prague Workshop, founded by Rudolf II of Hapsburg and entrusted to the Florentine Castrucci family.

11. *Abraham's banquet,* after a design by Bernardino Poccetti, 1610–1620 (* p. 67)

12. Grand-ducal manufacture, *Finials for a four-poster bed,* 17th cent., semi-precious stones and gilded bronze
Together with two other identical parts, these pieces crowned the columns of one of the semi-precious stone and precious metal beds which are now lost but were among the most admired pieces of furniture in the Florentine royal palace in the 17th cent.

13. Prague manufacture, *Table cabinet with landscapes,* early 17th cent. (* p. 68)

14. *Large cabinet with naturalistic mosaics,* 17th cent. (* p. 69)

15. Grand-ducal manufacture, *Two table legs,* early 18th cent., ebony, bronze and semi-precious stones
Surviving parts of an elaborate semi-precious stone table support, some examples of this work can be found in Palazzo Pitti and other European collections.

16–17. Grand-ducal manufacture, Various carved semi-precious stones, early 18th cent.
These unfinished carvings were destined to decorate reliquaries, sacred furnishings and furniture like cases and cabinets.

18. *Eight landscape views,* early 18th cent. (* p. 70)

IV/8

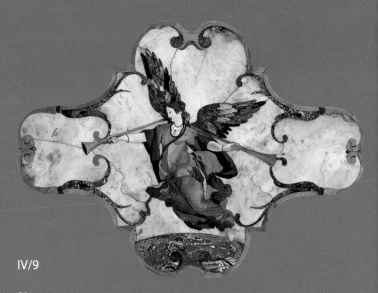

IV/9

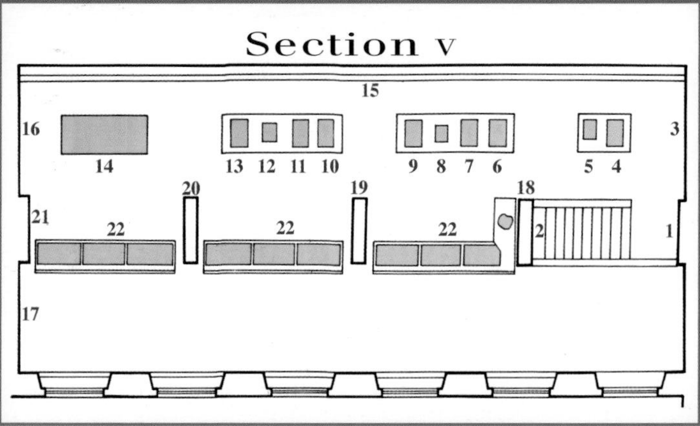

THE SEMI-PRECIOUS STONE WORKSHOP

The beauty and enhanced value of these miraculous creations derives from a skilful and demanding operative procedure. The artists' or sculptors' imagination came to life in a base design for the semi-precious stone craftsmen. The craftsmen then transposed it into the chromatic and expressive language of the stones using their own creative expertise. Thus an almost unlimited selection of stones were laid out allowing the creator, with a sure and patient eye, to choose the most appropriate colour nuances for the subject. The Medici sent for the stones from all over the known world, over 600 samples are displayed here showing the abundance and variety of the materials kept in stock. Another evocative reminder of the Workshop's activities are the work benches: the more simple style was intended for the mosaic work and entrusted the object's outcome to the practised dexterity of the creator, while the 18th-century style is more 'technological' and was used for the different types of ductile shaping work ('intaglio plastico').

Paintings

(At the top of the stairs)

1. Domenico Remps, *Trompe-l'œil still life*, 1650–1700 (* p. 71)

(Above the stair well)

2. Giovan Battista Giorgi, *Shell and coral composition*, ca 1820, oil on canvas

Design for a semi-precious stone table in the Royal Palace of Naples.

(Entrance wall from bottom)

3a. Antonio Cioci, *Two still life compositions with Ginori and oriental porcelain*, 1785–1786, oil on canvas

Designs for two semi-precious stone table tops at Palazzo Pitti.

3b. Antonio Cioci, *Two still life compositions with antique vases*, ca 1785, oil on canvas

Designs as above.

Workbenches

4. *Workbench for glyptics*, 1750-1800 (* p. 73)

5. *Bench for small-scale carving work*, 18th and 19th cent., wood

6. *Bench for carving*, 18th cent., wood

7. *Bench for carving with a movable shaft*, 18th cent., wood

The shaft which held the tools could be angled according to the requirements of the cut.

8. *Bench for Florentine mosaics*, 19th cent., wood

According to a design which has remained the same since the 16th cent., the bench is composed of a grip to block the piece of stone in place and a little saw made of soft iron. The cutting action of the iron saw is aided by a humid abrasive substance.

9. *Bench for carving*, 18th and 19th centuries, wood

10. *Bench for large scale carving*, 18th cent.

11. *Elliptic beam compass*, 19th cent.

Tool for cutting elliptic shapes of various dimensions on flat slabs.

12. *Bench for carving*, 18th and 19th centuries, wood

13. *Bench for small-scale carving work*, 19th cent., wood

14. Display cabinet with different cutting and shaping tools

You can see various 19th-cent. tools here which were mostly conceived to aid the cut, incision or carving of semi-precious stones. They were designed and made for specific use inside the Workshop. If you open the drawers you can see some examples of 19th-cent. graphics tests. These tests were done for the entrance exam to become an apprentice in the old Medici Workshop.

15. Semi-precious stone sample collection (* p. 72)

(On the long wall)

Paintings

(End wall and on the left)

16. Antonio Cioci, *Two compositions of shells, coral and pearls*, 1783–1784, oil on canvas

Designs for a pair of semi-precious stone table tops at Palazzo Pitti.

17. Antonio Cioci, *Two still life compositions with antique vases*, ca 1780, oil on canvas

Designs as above

(On the columns from the left)

18. Giuseppe Zocchi, *Two views of ruins with figures*, 1751, oil on canvas (fig. p. 32)

Like the paintings between the windows and on the pillars on the ground floor, these are designs for works in semi-precious stones destined for the Viennese residence of Francesco Stefano of Lorraine.

19. Giuseppe Zocchi, *Six game scenes: Playing on a swing, Badminton, Pelota, Archery* (fig. p. 33), *Billiards, Tennis*, 1751–1752, oil on canvas

20. Giuseppe Zocchi, *The hours of the day: Morning* (fig. p. 32), *Midday* (* p. 76), *After Lunch, Night, Night*, 1753–1755, oil on canvas

The artist painted two versions of *Night* but only one was transposed into semi-precious stones.

21. Giuseppe Zocchi, *The senses: Sight, Hearing, Taste, Smell*, 1751, oil on canvas

22. Display cabinets on the balcony: examples of Workshop's activities

In the cabinets on the edge of the mezzanine level you can see the main production phases of a Florentine mosaic (* p. 74) and an 'intaglio' in semi-precious stones; various 18th- and 19th-cent. fragments of mosaics and unfinished carving work; documents and memorabilia from the Opificio activities, for example a map of chalcedony deposits in the Volterra area; a register of all the works sold to the public in the late 19th cent.; an album with the signatures of famous visitors, etc. In the drawers under the cabinets there is a series of watercolour drawings from the late 18th cent. to the early 19th cent. These were used as designs for tables, snuffboxes (* p. 75), jewels and other objects in semi-precious stones created during the same period by the Workshop. (fig. p. 33).

V/4

V/5

V/6

31

V/18

V/20 *Morning*

V/19 *Archery*

V/22 *Portrait and Entry into Florence of Grand Duke Francesco Stefano of Lorraine,* chalcedony cameo

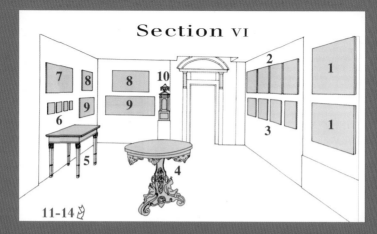

Section VI

11-14

THE LORRAINE PERIOD

The Hapsburg Lorraine family succeeded the Medici and reigned in Tuscany between 1737 and 1858. It maintained the court Workshop which demonstrated that it was able to adapt its repertoire to the highly regarded, more classical 18th-century taste. The Workshop abandoned the naturalistic mosaic decoration linked to the Baroque. Semi-precious stone mosaics featuring landscapes with ruins and scenes of 18th-century life came into fashion. A lighter, gauzy palette consistent with rococo tastes was used. Giuseppe Zocchi, a Florentine artist, contributed to these changes by working regularly with the Workshop. He produced a series of over 60 paintings which have remained at the Opificio. They were all designs ready to be brilliantly transposed into semi-precious stone works, destined for the Imperial Palace in Vienna. When neoclassicism became fashionable it influenced the Workshop's work throughout the 19th century, figures were abandoned in favour of sophisticated still life compositions with shells or classic emblems. These were also combined with floral themes which became popular again during the century.

1. Giuseppe Zocchi, *Allegories of Air* (fig. p. 36) *and Water*, 1760–1765, oil on canvas

Two designs for semi-precious stone mosaic tables destined for the Viennese imperial court. Today they are divided between the Hofburg in Vienna and the Louvre in Paris.

2. *The Arts: Painting, Music* (* p. 77), *Sculpture and Architecture* from the design by Giuseppe Zocchi, 1776–1780, semi-precious stones

3. Giuseppe Zocchi, *The Arts: Painting* (fig. p. 36), *Music, Sculpture and Architecture*, 1752, oil on canvas

In the series of designs prepared by Zocchi for Vienna *The Arts* were particularly popular and were replicated several times in semi-precious stones.

4. *Table with a garland of roses and shells*, after a design by Giovan Battista Giorgi, 1860,

semi-precious stone table top on carved, gilded wooden feet (fig. p. 12)

5. *Table top in porphyry with musical instruments and garland* (* p. 79)

6. Gesualdo Ferri, *Emblems of the Arts*, 1778, oil on canvas (fig. p. 37)

When the four *Arts* were replicated for Pietro Leopoldo (no. 2) a new frame was designed by the artist Ferri, who did these still life designs for the corners.

7. Giovan Battista Giorgi, *Garland and musical instruments*, ca 1840, oil on canvas

Design for at table top (no. 5), in Neoclassic-Romantic style

8 *Two Views of Rome:* the *Pantheon* and the *Tomb of Cecilia Metella*, from designs by Ferdinando Partini, ca 1797 and ca 1860, semi-precious stone mosaic (* p. 80)

This second work is a faithful replica of the 18th-cent. original made by the Workshop. It was given to Pope Pius IX in 1857 and is now in Somerset House in London.

9. *Two table tops with a still life of shells*, after a design by Carlo Carlieri, ca 1816, semi-precious stone mosaic on antique red porphyry

The evocative, decorative theme invented by Zocchi (no. 1) was a popular choice for the Workshop's mosaics and remained fashionable until almost halfway through the 19th cent.

10. *Ciborium*, after a design by Cosimo Siries, ca 1787, semi-precious stones and gilded bronze

This ciborium was designed by the goldsmith and bronze worker Siries who was director of the Workshop at the time. It was part of an 18th-cent. altar for the Villa del Poggio Imperiale that was dismantled a few decades later.

Series of panels with various subjects

(Behind the arch)

11. *Two landscapes*, 18th cent., semi-precious stone relief

12. *Four figures*, of peasants and townsfolk, late 18th cent., soft stone mosaic

13. *Two landscapes with figures*, 18th cent., soft stone mosaic

14. *Little dog*, semi-precious stone mosaic on nephrite, 18th cent. (fig. p. 57)

VI/1 *Allegory of Air*

VI/3 *Painting*

VI/3

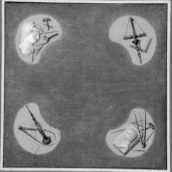

VI/6

VI/14

Section VII

SIMILAR GENRES: PAINTING ON STONE AND 'SCAGLIOLA'

The lasting success of the semi-precious stones in Florence paved the way for other similar forms of artistic expression. This was the case of paintings on stone, a painting genre which found widespread success in the first half of the 17th century and had particularly good fortune at Cosimo II de' Medici's court. The paintings made for the Grand Duke by the cosmopolitan circle of artists at court almost always had the same base: the 'Arno' stone. This limestone was particularly appreciated for its beautiful markings as they evoked uneven, rocky landscapes and undulating seas. Allowing themselves to be guided by nature, the artists completed the picture using the stone's features as much as their own creative flair. The 'scagliola' was done on 'soft' gesso but was often inspired by the semi-precious stones for the effect it wanted to achieve. The base material was plain but the difficult technique used to finish the work ennobled it and was similar to that of marquetry. The 'scagliola' was fashionable mainly in the 18th century for tables or decorative framed works with views or copies from famous pictures using refined pictorial techniques. Many were done by the two great masters of the genre, Enrico Hugford, a monk from Vallombrosa and his pupil, Lamberto Cristiano Gori.

'Scagliole' (right hand wall)

1. Lamberto Cristiano Gori, *Our Lady of sorrows*, before 1777, 'scagliola' technique

Copy after a painting thought at the time to be by Guido Reni.

2, 3, 4. Lamberto Cristiano Gori, *Flowers, butterflies and insects*, 1778, 1782, 1784, 'scagliola' technique, (fig. p. 41)

5, 6, 7, 14, 15, 22, 23. Enrico Hugford, *Landscapes with rivers and coastal views*, ca mid 18th cent., (* p. 80)

The monk from Valombrosa Enrico Hugford was a gifted 'scagliola' maker and inventor of a technique which gave the 'scagliola' a delicate pictorial finish.

8, 17, 18. Enrico Hugford's circle of

artists, *Coastal land-scapes*, ca 1750–1800, 'scagliola' technique

9. Lamberto Cristiano Gori, *Landscape with knights*, 1763, 'scagliola' technique

10. Tuscan artist, *Landscape*, 18th cent., 'scagliola' technique

11, 12. Giuseppe Cianchi, *Coastal land-scapes*, ca mid 18th cent., 'scagliola' technique

The creator probably worked in Leghorn as the art of 'scagliola' was very popular there. He special-ised in views of the town.

13, 21. Giuseppe Cianchi, *Views of the Leghorn canal*, ca mid 18th cent., 'scagliola' technique

16. Tuscan artist, *Bambocciade* (style of painting scenes from real life), 18th cent., 'scagliola' technique

19, 20. Giuseppe Cianchi, *Views of the port*, ca mid 18th cent., 'scagliola' technique

24. *Portrait of Enrico Hugford*, after a design by Lamberto Cristiano Gori, 1757, engraving

(On the same wall)
Table top with musi-cal instruments and flowers, after a design by Niccolò Betti, 1874, semi-precious stone mosaic on black Bel-gian marble

The table top was pro-duced by the Opificio

after the end of the Grand Duchy of Tuscany.

Casket with *Pallas Athena and the Miracles of Christ*, before 1624, ebony, gilded bronze and oil painting on lapis lazuli, Augsburg

This is an example of the precious ornaments using several materials that the workshops in the Bavarian town specialised in. In 1624 it was already among the Medici orna-ments at the Villa del Pog-gio Imperiale.

Paintings on stone (left hand side)
25, 26. *Slabs of 'pietra paesina'* (a marbled limestone), 18th cent.

The Arno stone evoked rocky landscapes and was also admired when framed on its own.

27, 28, 31. Filippo Napoletano's circle of artists, *Seashore with galleons*, ca 1620, oil on 'alberese' limestone

This stone was called 'lined Arno' for its evoca-tive aquatic aspect.

29, 30. *Naval battles*, ca 1600–1625, oil on 'lined Arno' stone

32. Filippo Napoletano, *St. Augustine's vision*, ca 1620, oil on 'lined Arno' stone

33. *Monk with a don-key*, ca 1600–1625, oil on 'pietra paesina'

34. *Jonah and the whale* (* p. 82)

35. *Mary Magdalene in the desert*, ca 1600–1625, oil on 'pietra paesina'

36. Francesco Ligozzi, *Dante and Virgil in Hell*, 1620, oil on 'pietra paesina' (fig. p. 40)

(On the same wall)
Table with musical in-struments and flowers, after a design by Nic-colò Betti, 1868, semi-precious stone mosaic on an ebony base

(Entrance wall)
37. Cornelius Van Poelenburgh, *Latona turning the Lycean shepherds into frogs*, ca 1620, oil on lapis lazuli

38, 39. *Olympia and Bireno* and *Ruggero and Angelica* (fig. p. 40), ca 1600–1625, oil on 'pietra paesina'

40, 41. *Two episodes from "Orlando in Love"*, ca 1600–1625, oil on 'pietra paesina'

VII/36

VII/39

VII/2

THE OPIFICIO DELLE PIETRE DURE
AFTER THE UNIFICATION OF ITALY

When the Kingdom of Italy (1861) was formed the Opificio acquired the name it still has today but, with the local court no longer in existence to support its aristocratic art, it had to support itself in other ways and find new buyers for its creations. The Workshop chose to concentrate on floral themes which were coming back into fashion in applied arts during the second half of the 19th century. The Opificio dealt with these themes with a creativity and elegance reminiscent of the great traditions of the past. Unfortunately, it was their high quality and therefore the commitment they required for their creation which made them very uncompetitive next to the more 'mass produced' products by various semi-precious stone workshops in Florence at the time. The director of the Opificio, Edoardo Marchionni, was the artist behind some exquisite designs for mosaics in the 1870s and 1880s and as some remained unsold, they now provide information for the Museum on this exceptional but unlucky final chapter of the Workshop. At the end of the 19th century artistic creation had almost completely been abandoned in order to start a new activity which would keep the old technical knowledge alive. The Opificio was devoted from that point onwards to the restoration of artistic heritage.

1. *Table with flowers, fruit, birds and grape vines* (* p. 83)

2. Paolo Ricci, *Dante Alighieri*, 1877, semi-precious stone sculpture

Sculptures in semi-precious stones were the pride of the grand-ducal Workshop in the 17th cent. and early 18th cent. They became popular again in the last period of activity thanks to the astounding ability of the 'intagliatore' (semi-precious stone sculptor), Paolo Ricci (no. 5).

3. Ottaviano Giovannozzi, *Leopoldo II of Hapsburg Lorraine*, 1832, marble bust

This is a young image of the last Grand Duke of Tuscany who was given the nickname 'Canapone' (hempen rope) by the Florentines because of his blond hair.

4. *Elisa Bonaparte Baciocchi*, after a design by Lorenzo Bartolini, 1810, marble bust

Napoleon's sister protected and enlarged the semi-precious stone Workshop during her time in Florence as sovereign of Tuscany (1809–1814).

5. Paolo Ricci, *Cimabue*, 1874, semi-precious stone sculpture

The new Kingdom of Italy celebrated its illustrious men in town squares with statues while the Opificio made smaller, more precious monuments in semi-precious stones (no. 2).

VIII/1/5

45

Section VIII
Room 2

1. *Flower stand* (* p. 86)

2. Florentine manufacture, *Table top with flowers, birds and a string of pearls*, ca 1850–1900, semi-precious stone mosaic on black Belgian marble

This table top has recently been acquired by the Museum and is the work of one of the private workshops in Florence in the second half of the 19th cent. It elegantly imitates the grand-ducal designs of the 17th cent.

3. *Series of panels with fruit and flowers*, ca 1875–1900, semi-precious stone mosaic

(Wall between the two windows)

4. Edoardo Marchionni, *Self-Portrait*, late 19th cent., oil on canvas

Marchionni was the director of the Opificio for several years and created many designs for semi-precious stones. He also worked as an artist in his own right.

5. *Frame with flowers*, after a design by Edoardo Marchionni, 1886–1887, semi-precious stone mosaic

This is an example a 'minor' piece in terms of its size, but not in terms of its exquisite inventive charm.

6. *Album with the Savoy family coat of arms*, ca 1870, semi-precious stone mosaic and velvet

Inside this album there is a rare collection of photographic images of the Holy Land taken by the Duke of Aosta.

7. *Two caskets*, 1877–1878, ebony and semi-precious stones

8. *Four samples for wall coverings*, 1881–1882, soft stone mosaic

The Opificio offered their clients ambitious mosaic wall coverings of extraordinary decorative impact albeit made with less expensive soft stones.

9. *Panels with flowers*, ca 1875–1900, semi-precious stone mosaic

Table tops
(Wall opposite the window)

Twenty table tops, destined for the public but never sold, have remained in the Opificio from the period between 1864 and 1885. They are all in semi-precious stone mosaics and mainly show floral decorations on black backgrounds; the oldest ones are based on designs by Niccolò Betti, director of the Opificio until 1876. The later ones are based on designs by Edoardo Marchionni (no. 6) and show precocious signs of the *Art Nouveau* style.

1. *Doves and ornaments*, 1870

This is a 'classic' theme which became popular again after the discovery of the Pompei mosaics and remained so during the 19th cent.

2. *Garlands of vine leaves and grapes*, 1871

This table doesn't use the normal central decorative motif but is circled by a sophisticated vine leaf design with soft autumnal colours.

3. *Goblet and fruit tree saplings*, 1878 (fig. on title page)

The naturalistic decoration is enhanced by the octagonal composition.

4. *Dantesque emblems and geranium shoots*, 1873

The central decoration is a little affected but the design and colours on the previously unseen, domestic garland of geraniums are extremely refined.

5. *Magnolias and morning glory*, 1877

This is one of the first and most successful works by Edoardo Marchionni, it anticipates the naturalism of the Art Nouveau style and the Japanese tastes which influenced European art at the end of the century.

6. *Fruit composition*, 1864

7. *Ivy, cameo and pearls*, 1873

The vegetation combines with the *trompe-l'œil* effect of the jewel left on the table top

8. *Bacchic emblems and flowers*, 1873

The composition of musical instruments was one of the favourite decorations of the Neoclassic period and can be seen again here with vine-shoots which are both scrupulously naturalistic and creative.

9. *Grapes and vine leaves*, Sicilian jasper and translucent chalcedony, 1865 (fig. p. 46)

This is a magical 'reinvention' of the familiar subject of grapes

10. *Bracelet, pearls and camellia*, 1875 (fig. p. 46)

This could be the table top where the *Dame aux Camélias*, made famous by Dumas fils, left her seductive ornaments on her return from a mundane evening out

Table tops nos. 11–20 follow in Room 3.

VIII/2/9

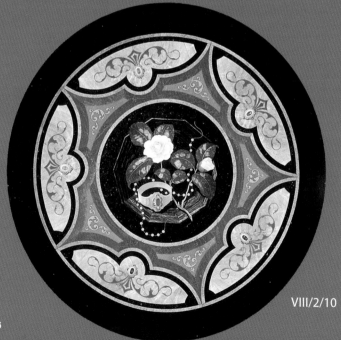

VIII/2/10

Section VIII Room 3

1. *Large vase with flowers and animals*, 1882-1888, semi-precious stone mosaic (fig. p. 48)

This ornamental vase was designed to demonstrate the Opificio's creative flair and technical skill but it was never finished. This spectacular style of work no loner suited the period so the Opificio turned to the new activity of restoration.

2. *Panel with a large vase of flowers* (* p. 87)

This was an ambitious design by Edoardo Marchionni conceived as a covering for a wardrobe door.

3. *Gueridon*, Table top, 1860-1870, semi-precious stones on gilded metal legs (fig. p. 49)

This is an elegant variation on the theme of still life with vases which had been enormously popular in the Workshop's mosaics at the end of the 18th cent.

4. Two panels with still life, late 19th cent., semi-precious stone mosaic

5. Table top, 1882, semi-precious stones on porphyry

6. *Italy set free*, ca 1880, sculpture in semi-precious stones; next, its model in coloured gesso

This work is not completely finished but celebrates the wars of Independence and the acquisition of Venice in 1866.

7. *Shepherds resting*, ca 1870, semi-precious stone mosaic

8. Display cabinet with various objects in semi-precious stones:

(From top to bottom, from left to right)

First part:

- *Paperweight*, 1878-1879, semi-precious stone mosaic

- *Paperweight with a gardenia*, 1878-1879, semi-precious stone relief

- *Ornaments for guns*, ca 1880, agate on slate

- *Paperweight with fruit in relief*, late 19th cent., semi-precious stones

- *Paperweight with flowers*, late 19th cent., semi-precious stone mosaic

- *Binding for a Massbook*, ca 1875-1900, soft stones and leather

- *Paper cutter and various writing desk accessories*, late 19th cent., semi-precious stones

With the aim of increasing its sales to the public the Opificio started producing small, less expensive objects at the end of the 19th cent.

- *Etruscan style cup*, 1878, porphyry

This ancient Egyptian stone, an imperial symbol of ancient Rome, became popular again in the Neoclassic era and remained so throughout the 19th cent.

- *Ink stand*, 1878, porphyry

Second part:

- *Two paperweights with portraits of Michelangelo*, 1878, semi-precious stone in relief

The quality of these two medals leads us to believe they are by Paolo Ricci, the gifted 'intagliatore' (semi-precious stone sculptor) who worked for the Opificio in the second half of the 19th cent.

- *Vase with a serpent*, 1885, basaltic rock

- *Two neo-Renaissance goblets*, semi-precious stones with metal binding and enamels, 1863

- *Goblet*, 1880, jasper

- *Goblet on a base*, 1880, semi-precious stones

- *Vase with a dragon*, 1885, basaltic rock

The exoticism of the end of the century influenced the form of the vases which were inspired by Chinese designs.

- *Recipient for liquid*, 1882, chalcedony

This and the two objects that follow reflect the sophisticated, sober Japanese tastes which influenced applied arts in Europe in the last decades of the 19th cent.

- *Cup*, 1882, chalcedony

- *Little jar with a lid*, 1882, chalcedony (fig. p. 49)

- *Vase with a single handle*, ca 1845, porphyry

- *Etruscan-style cup*, 1863, porphyry

VIII/3/1

VIII/3/3

VIII/3/8 *Little jar with a lid* (display cabinet)

Table tops (wall opposite the window)

11. *Magnolias, roses and convolvuli*, 1881

12. *Tulips and flowers*, 1882

13. *Roses and sage*, 1876

14. *Tea roses and convolvuli*, 1885

15. *Roses and wild flowers*, 1881

16. *Roses and bellflowers*, 1878

17. *Azaleas and roses*, 1877

18. *Bowl with flowers*, 1874 (fig. p. 51)

19. *Butterflies*, second half of the 19th century

20. *Convolvuli and hemerocallis*,1880 (fig. on the right)

VIII/3/20

VIII/3/18

The masterpieces

◀◀p. 17, no. 8

Portrait of Cosimo I de' Medici

The stone image of the first Grand Duke was based on a design painted on canvas, also present in the Museum, by Domenico Passignano. From the very beginning of the Workshop and in the centuries that followed, it was custom to entrust the most accredited artists at court with the preparation of the design. The semi-precious stone craftsmen would then interpret the design, skilfully using the natural chromatic palette of the stones. This portrait was commissioned by Ferdinando I for his father's grave and the stones which form the Cosimo's image are all from the local area as a mark of respect to the Grand Duke from the Tuscan land. An artist from Fiesole, Francesco Ferrucci, created this mosaic dated 1598. He was one of the first specialists of the stone mosaic inlay technique ('commesso lapideo') in the Workshop, founded ten years earlier by Ferdinando I.

◀◀ p. 17, no. 15

Large vase of flowers

After the first 'commessi' with their geometric and abstract decoration the craftsmen at the Workshop, even before the end of the 16th century, were already able to produce more complex images. These were obtained by cutting sections of stone with painstaking precision then fitting them perfectly together in such a way as to give the illusion of a complete image. These two large panels are among the first and already sublime creations of the kind. They were originally in a series of 12 panels from the decoration of a small oratory in the Medici Villa of Poggio Imperiale. The floral theme makes one of its first appearances here and was to remain one of the favourite subjects for the Florentine mosaics throughout the 17th century. Both archaeological marble and semi-precious stones can be seen in the exquisite and varied stone palette. The attractive artifice of the central *lilium* is particularly noteworthy as the luminous and col-

our changing surface of the oriental chalcedony lets a thin, metallic layer shine through.

◀◀ p. 17, no. 17

Table top with a parrot, flowers and military trophies

Among the stone furniture made with the new mosaic technique in the late 16th century table tops featured prominently. They were sumptuous pieces of furniture which became the pride of both princes and collectors. The oldest tables, made according to Vasari's designs for the Medici, had abstract decorations while the new style, preferred by Ferdinando I de' Medici, used figurative subjects. This table is from Ferdinando's era and would have been to his taste. The bright colours of the archaeological marble from ancient Rome stand out against the black background, an aspect which became standard for the Florentine mosaics during the 17th century. The technique was used to make complex compositions of pseudo-classical emblems and naturalistic subjects, both styles were destined to become lasting themes in the grand-ducal Workshop in Florence. The table tops were made like a big puzzle where even the base layer, seemingly whole, was formed with various sections of shaped and perfectly joined black, Belgian marble.

◀◀ p. 20, no. 1

Design for the Cappella dei Principi

A funerary mausoleum worthy of the Medici dynasty had been planned by Cosimo I and Francesco I but was actually built by Ferdinando I in 1604. He wanted it to be architecturally spectacular with the inside entirely covered in semiprecious stones. The project was started with great enthusiasm and commitment by the grand-ducal Workshop but everything slowed down in the second half of the 17th century. It was still unfinished in 1743, the year in which this design was made by order of Anna Maria Luisa de' Medici. The Palatine Electress was aware that the Medici family would die out with her so she aimed to finish the tambour and the dome exactly as they are shown in this design with marble and frescos. Unfortunately, in that same year the last member of the Medici family died and the chapel was finished almost a century later by the Grand Dukes of Lorraine.

◄◄ p. 20, no. 2

Tuscan town coat of arms

The wide wainscot which circles the inside of the Cappella dei Principi is decorated with joined panels alternating large vase shapes in semi-precious stones with coats of arms from the towns in the Grand Duchy of Tuscany. They are framed in an elegant, late Mannerism style.

Well before the construction started on the chapel in 1604, the grand-ducal Workshop was already preparing the difficult internal decoration. The very first works to be prepared were the coats of arms which are known to have been worked on as early as 1589. They were conceived as standards on which stood the heraldic emblem of the town. The coats of arms have a white marble background which gives them an anything but funereal luminosity and enhances the ancient marble's spring colours and iridescent mother of pearl. The panel here in the Museum was made when the coat of arms series was finished inside the chapel and is probably a copy which would have served as a substitute if the original had to be restored.

◄◄p. 21, no. 10

Elijah and the angel

In the centre of the octagonal structure of the Cappella dei Principi there should have been a temple-like altar covered in semi-precious stones, crowned by a righteous rock crystal dome and bound together with precious metals like a jewel in a precious case. The mounting of such a wondrous design occupied the grand-ducal Workshop for the first half of the 17th century but it never succeeded in finishing the sparkling temple. It remained in the workshops until it was disassembled in the 18th century. Among the decorations acquired by the Museum of the Opificio there are a series of panels showing sacred stories. These panels, based on elaborate designs by various artists working for the Medici court, have been transposed into fascinating 'paintings of stone'. This biblical scene, made in 1612, shows the angel reviving the prophet Elijah. They are set in a landscape with a small, homely chapel and a cypress tree.

Tuscan landscape

This view of the Tuscan hills, destined for the Cappella dei Princici along with another similar landscape, gives the impression that it was done on the spot with the small crouching hare in the foreground and the loaded donkey ambling along next to the traveller. The work was done in semi-precious stones in 1608 and was based on a design by Bernardino Poccetti, a distinguished Mannerist painter of the Medici court. In this case the artist reveals himself to be precociously open to the new naturalistic style of the 17th century. The craftsman's pictorial sensibility is masterly in this semi-precious stone mosaic, the Sicilian jasper has been chosen carefully for its various colour gradations in order to enhance the shadowy hills in the foreground. The brighter tones show through from the distance under a sky dotted with clouds.

◄◄p. 21, no. 12

◀◀ p. 23, no. 2

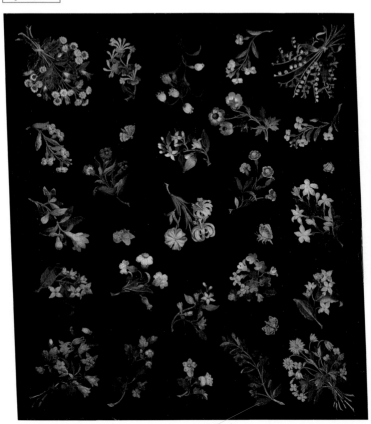

Design for a table top with flowers

A variety of themes were tackled by the grand-ducal 'commessi' in the first years of the Workshop but from the second decade of the 17th century, a prevalently naturalistic repertoire was established. This included compositions of flowers and fruit, often combined with birds and became the distinctive *leitmotiv* of the Florentine mosaics. The instigator of this popular style was the artist Iacopo Ligozzi, whose exquisite gift for observation of the natural world had already produced a series of graceful botanical and zoological tables for Francesco I de Medici. Many semi-precious stone works have been linked to him, but this oil on paper painting is all that is left of his preparatory designs. The painting was for a table, of unknown whereabouts, featuring a bunch of flowers brought to life by the use of vivid colours on a nocturnal background of Flemish yardstick.

Panel with a sunflower

The attractive theme of sunflowers was often seen in the Workshop and the Museum also has a second version in semi-precious stones. The most beautiful panel is the one you can see here, composed of less valuable limestone and signed on the back by Gerolamo della Valle in 1664. The inventive choice of the soft Arno jasper and its nuances lights up the radiant corolla (inner part of the flower) and makes the leaves change colour while the speckled alabaster makes the wings of the two butterflies seem as if they are actually beating. Like many of the other single, unused panels in the Museum this one with the sunflower was destined for the external decoration of a wooden cabinet.

Parrot on a pear tree

This panel, which stands alone, was probably destined to become the door of a cabinet. It was normal practice in the Workshop to prepare series of panels in advance, mostly with naturalistic subjects. They could then be quickly mounted on wooden drawers or cabinets, both items were frequently made by the Workshop throughout the 17th century and beyond. In the varied ornithological repertoire introduced by the artist Iacopo Ligozzi, the image of parrots was among the favourites. This charming, exotic bird could be admired in the Boboli Gardens aviaries. It inspired the craftsmen with its chromatically brilliant, multicoloured plumage and led them to produce evocative interpretations from their semi-precious stone palette.

◀◀ p. 23, no. 1

◄◄ p. 26, no. 4

Cosimo III and Tuscany

In the era of the penulti-mate Grand Duke, Cosi-mo III (regent from 1670 to 1723), the Workshop devoted a large part of its time and consummate ability to the production of semi-precious stones in relief. This technique was particularly well suit-ed to the Baroque taste. The creator of this large chalcedony cameo was Giuseppe Antonio Tor-ricelli, an unsurpassed master of the *glyptics* (a type of sculpting work often used for cameos). The cameo has an unu-sual size and a famous subject almost as though it wants to rival the impe-rial cameos from Roman times. The composition is also pseudo-classical with the Grand Duke in antique armour standing before a female figure who symbolises Tusca-ny, both in front of a cir-cular temple dedicated to Peace. In addition to the smooth look of the 'intaglio' work which has supplely shaped the hard chalcedony, the clever use of the yellow veins in the rock to define the tree's trunk and foliage is to be admired. These ele-ments are absent from the medal which inspired the cameo but here the artist has used them to provide a scenic background.

◀◀ p. 27, no. 7

A bedroom holy water stoup

The 'intaglio' of semi-precious stones, using relief or rounded techniques, produced un- usual 'mosaic sculp- tures'. The single parts would be carved separately in differ- ent coloured stones then linked together to form a complete im- age with internal pins and glue. The tech- nique has been used on this stoup for the Angel and the Virgin where the two heads' chromatic and duc-

tile quality stands out. The chalcedony was carved from a single piece and used for its skin tones on the faces, and for its yellow veins on the blonde head of hair. The finesse of the semi-precious stone work was then improved and ennobled by the areas in gilded bronze which constitute an essential part of this style and are highly representative of the grand-ducal Workshop's luxurious creativity during Cosimo III's reign.

Abraham's banquet

The biblical story of Abraham, who meets three angels disguised as travellers, was destined for the unfinished, opulently decorated semi-precious stone altar of the Cappella dei Principi. The design was prepared in the early 17th century by Bernardino Poccetti but the transposition into semi-precious stones was done by the Florentine mosaic workshop set up in Prague (with Florentine craftsmen) by the Emperor Rudolf II of Hapsburg. It is probable the original design was also modified given that Abraham is wearing a bearskin and a fur cape which make him look like a Bohemian nobleman. The polychrome jaspers used to create the figures and landscapes also came from Bohemia and were habitually employed by the Imperial Workshop in Prague. Unlike the Florentine workshops, the one in Prague only used jasper as the bohemian lands were rich in the material.

◀◀p. 27, no. 13

Table cabinet with landscapes

The Florentine mosaic Workshop, created in imitation of the Medici Workshop by Rudolf II of Hapsburg, was active for entire first quarter of the 17th century. This table cabinet, sent as a gift to the Grand Duke in Florence, was among its creations and has an ingenious design. To open it you must turn the little column on the left of the door revealing a central compartment with four small drawers. Other drawers can be pulled out from the bottom where there is a back gammon game (called *tric-trac* at the time). It was removed using two gilded silver handles ('tiretti'). The outside has been embellished with panels of semi-precious stone mosaics featuring landscapes, the favoured subject of the Prague Workshop.

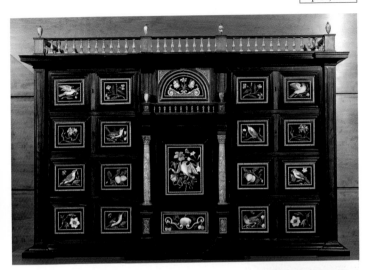
Large cabinet with naturalistic mosaics

Cabinets were among the most appreciated pieces of furniture by the collectors between the 16th and 17th centuries. They were seen as decorative and functional, destined to act as safes to keep precious collections, jewels, medals, coins and cameos etc. The exterior appearance also reflected the value of the contents, in Florence the cabinets were almost always distinguished with semi-precious stones arranged in panels on the doors and drawers. During the 17th century the grand-ducal Workshop produced a large quantity of these pieces of furniture, all destined for Medici palaces or sent as gifts to illustrious people. The size and structure of the pieces varied but they were often designed, as seen here, as miniature versions of monumental architectural façades, their calibrated and symmetrical forms perfectly in accordance with Florentine tastes. The darling naturalistic themes of flowers, fruit and birds were among the recurring subjects for the external mosaics as their preparatory designs could be transposed more than once, varying the choice of stones.

◀◀p. 27, no. 18

Eight landscape views

Between the 17th and 18th centuries the landscape subjects, popular at the start of the Workshop, came back into fashion. The scenes were mainly of rivers and lakes in simple, almost naïf compositions with a freshness enhanced by the presence of lively little figures. The chromatic range, based on luminous and translucent spring hues, contributes to these little genre scenes' charm. They were made in different sizes and had different destinations, cabinets, drawers, table tops, to hang on walls, panels for *boiseries* and decorative coverings for entire rooms. The baroque drawing rooms covered in semiprecious stones evoked in Palazzo Pitti have all been lost, but there is still a trace of the style at the Villa La Favorita in Rastatt in Germany. In 1720 an entire room was covered in mosaics made in Florence with landscape medallions very similar to those at the Museum.

◀◀ p. 29, no. 1

Trompe-l'œil still life

This unique painting comes from the inventories of the Medici collections and is recorded as a 'scarabattolo' or little wardrobe that opens in front of our eyes with insidious veracity to show us, and almost invite us, to touch the artistic and natural curiosities brought together there by an inquisitive collector. *Trompe-l'œil* paintings like this were conceived in a way as to generate the illusion of reality for the observer and were especially popular in the 17th century. The Flemish artists excelled in this technique as their artistic traditions encouraged a meticulous and analytical style in natural images. The painting is dedicated to marquis Riccardi whose address can be seen on the letter slipped under the glass, and was done by Domenico Remps, an artist from Antwerp who worked in Florence in the second half of the 17th century.

◀◀p. 30, no. 15

The semi-precious stone sample collection

The quality and value of the work created over three centuries in the grand-ducal Workshop was only made possible by extraordinary reserves of 'raw material' accumulated by the Medici. Cosimo I sent for porphyry and other ancient marbles from Rome, Francesco and Ferdinando, who shared the family passion for beautiful stones and passed it on to their descendants, preferred the clear and unalterable luminosity of the semi-precious stones. Ferdinando issued an edict to reserve the right to collect agate and chalcedony for the Grand Duke, two materials which were abundant in Tuscany. He also encouraged the acquisition and search for semi-precious stones all over the known world: Sicily, Corsica and Bohemia for jasper, Germany for agate, Persia for lapis lazuli and even further to the east, India for transparent chalcedony and blood agate from Goa. The Museum's sample collection, created when it was founded at the end of the 19th century, offers a comprehensive review of the variety and richness of the grand-ducal stone reserves. These reserves are so vast that in spite of widespread use over the centuries the collection is still abundant today.

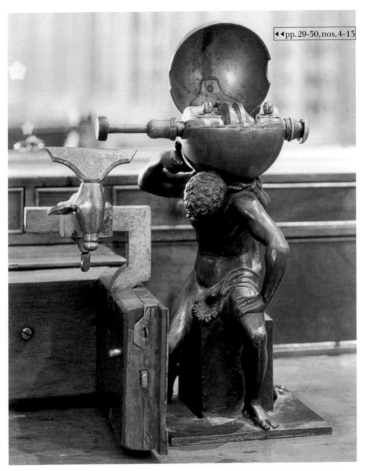
◀◀pp. 29-30, nos. 4-13

Workbench for glyptics

The Museum has a rare collection of 18th-century workbenches which were used in the grand-ducal Workshop for the carving of semi-precious stones. This one, decorated with a bronze statuette of *Atlas*, combines functionality and elegance. The horizon-tal shaft mechanism is equipped with a pulley linked to a pedal to con-trol the rotation and is concealed by the globe on the large curve of At-las' shoulder. The cutting tools, wheels or pointed instruments, are inserted into a holder in the shaft and are interchange-able depending on the requirements of the cut. The silica based semi-precious stones are then scratched and shaped using a rotary move-ment along with the in-dispensable aid of damp-ened abrasive dust. The work surface is shaped in order to provide a com-fortable support for the craftsman and to allow all the drawers, some of which were designed to hold the cutting tools, to be locked in one go.

◄◄ p. 31, no. 22

The production phases of a Florentine mosaic

The two cabinets display a summary of the laborious phases which culminate in the creation of a Florentine mosaic or 'commesso'. The process starts with the watercolour on paper design which is traced to mark out the different sections of the whole. To create colour gradations the pebble of semi-precious stone is cut into thin slices, the appropriate nuances are chosen then carved around the edges into sections with a small saw and an abrasive substance. The edges are then filed in order to guarantee a perfect join between the sections. The next step is to turn the sections over and burnish them from the back to level them down to the same thickness. Still working from the back, an invisible layer of slate and wax mixed with conifer resin is applied; the same mixture is used to glue the sections together. The final step is to give the semi-precious stones a lasting brilliance by gradually and repeatedly passing abrasive dust over the surface.

Designs for a snuff-box with a semi-precious stone mosaic

Throughout the course of the Workshop's long history the semi-precious stone 'commessi' were preceded by a design on a scale of 1:1 that the artists could do in either oil on canvas or watercolour on paper. The more fragile paper designs from the 16th and 17th centuries have almost all been lost, but the Museum has a copious amount of 18th- and 19th-century drawings in its archives. The artists working for the Work-shop had to submit their designs to the director and the grand-ducal court, as it was there that the finished works would go.

Production between the 18th and 19th centuries was especially rich and elegant. In addition to the traditional tables and other time consuming pieces of furniture, small luxurious objects and trinkets for personal elegance were made. These included sets of jewellery or snuff-boxes decorated with delicate mosaics inspired by the neoclassical style.

◀◀p. 31, no. 20

After lunch from a series of paintings showing *The hours of the day*

These five paintings were done between 1753 and 1755 by Giuseppe Zocchi, one of the most gifted artists of 18th-century Florence. During the middle decades of the century he often received commissions to prepare 'commessi' designs for the Workshop. Between 1750 and 1765 the Opificio took on an extensive and prestigious project: a series of over 60 semi-precious stone works based on designs by Zocchi and destined for the Viennese residence of the Emperor and Grand Duke of Tuscany, Francesco Stefano of Lorraine. Zocchi's designs remained here at the Opificio and were conceived as a sequence of allegorical themes or customs. In the case of this series the mundane ritual which regulates the different moments of a noblewoman's day is gracefully celebrated.

◀◀ p. 34, no. 2

Music, from the series showing *The Arts*

The 60 or so semi-precious stone works made for the Emperor of Austria between 1750 and 1765 all reached their Viennese destination, but the especially captivating series of the four arts (painting, architecture, sculpture and music) was replicated in Florence between 1776 and 1780 for the Grand Duke Pietro Leopoldo. The direct comparison between Giuseppe Zocchi's designs and the stone work allows the appreciation of both the artist's refreshing inventiveness and the semi-precious stone craftsman's fantastic freedom in interpreting the painted design. In the Florentine replicas the frames, previously in bronze, were made in semi-precious stones. The exquisite 'still life' objects in the corners allude to the different arts and were based on an innovative design by Gesualdo Ferri.

◀◀ p. 35, no. 5

Table top in porphyry with musical instruments and garland

This flat surface, made between 1842 and 1849, shows the persistent popularity of antique red porphyry. The material was reserved for 'imperial' use in ancient Rome but was fashionable throughout the ages which were particularly attached to the classic model. After its popularity during the Renaissance it was taken up again by Neoclassicism and widely used by the craftsmen in the last decades of the 18th century until more than half way through the following century. This table is among the last important works for the close to extinct Florentine court. It is neoclassical in style, partly demonstrated by the intertwining of the central emblems, but the dazzling garland of flowers foretells the naturalistic tastes which were to dictate all of the middle and late 18th-century work.

◄◄ p. 35, no. 8

View of the Pantheon

This semi-precious stone work, set in the subdued and refined chromatic harmony of chalcedony and petrified stone (wood which has become stone by chemical alteration over time), is part of a series of six views of Rome prepared at the end of the 18th century for the Palazzo Pitti. The Workshop was attentive to the evolution of contemporary tastes and was constantly updating its repertoire. In the neoclassical period it substituted Zocchi's vivacious little scenes with sedate views of Rome. The pictorial designs for the *Views of Rome* were inspired by Piranesi's famous incisions and painted by Ferdinando Partini but figures were added by the more talented artist Giovan Battista Dell'Era in order to make them livelier. As always, the transposition into semi-precious stones is masterly in its choice and enhancement of the material's chromatic palette.

Landscape with a river

Along with other similar 'scagliole' in the Museum collections, this is the work of the Vallombrosa monk Enrico Hugford, an acknowledged master of the 'scagliola' technique in 18th-century Tuscany. These works were made from inexpensive gesso but the technique used to produce them, a mix between inlay work (marquetry) and frescos, was skilful and difficult. Thin layers were carved out of a prepared gesso slab according to the different chromatic areas. Next, variously

◄◄p. 38, no. 15

coloured liquid gessoes were poured into the cavities, penetrating the slab beneath to acquire stability. The scagliola's surface was then ready to be polished using animal glue, a technique which gave it a brilliant finish similar to that of marble or, in this case, of a delicate pastel under glass. Tuscany was rich in polychrome stones so the scagliola was not a very practical substitute for the marble marquetry but was more of a pictorial imitation genre, useful for tables and decorative works to hang on walls.

◀◀p. 39, no. 34

Jonah and the whale

The passion for the artistic use of stones which found so much popularity in the Medici court is well represented on this panel. This oil painting, done by Filippo Napoletano on a slab of stone is framed by a 'commesso' scroll of polychrome marbles. Painting on stone was a very popular genre from the end of the 16th century all through the 17th century. It was not exclusive to Florence but had a privileged place in the court of Cosimo II de' Medici. Artists from different places contributed to the court's vitality in this field. The late Mannerist and then Baroque tastes appreciated this type of work for the competition between the stones' natural patterns and the artist's creativity as he completed the appearance and the images suggested by the material with a brush. In this case the 'lined Arno' stone constitutes the base slab, evoking the flowing movement of the sea with its wavy lines and creating the artist's setting for the biblical scene of Jonah being saved from the whale's stomach.

Table with flowers, fruit, birds and grape vines

◀◀ p. 42, no. 1

The end of the Grand Duchy of Tuscany was imminent when this table was finished in 1855 and it was probably the Opificio's last large creation. The Grand Duke Ferdinando III of Hapsburg Lorraine was so satisfied with it he decided to give an additional bonus to the creator of the design and director of the work, Niccolò Betti. The renewal of the Florentine mosaic style is partly due to this refined artist. Thanks to his ideas, people abandoned the decorative repertoires based on neoclassical emblems which had been in use for so long. The return of the triumphal naturalistic themes, dear to the Florentine mosaics throughout the 17th century and beyond, can be seen on this circular table top. This time the theme appears with the floral and chromatic luxuriance which was characteristic of painting and applied arts in the late 19th century. Harmonious composition, the natural design and the radiant splendour of the colours all contribute to the table top's charm. It also has an appropriately important base made from sculpted, gilded wood. The botanical designs spread over this table top were used as a base for numerous variations on the floral theme that were made in the following decades and can be seen in the last two rooms of the Museum.

◀◀p. 44, no. 1

in black chalcedony. Large oriental masks cut from red jasper stand out on the edges while the mosaic panels on the four sides reveal the pictorial talent of the design's creator, Edoardo Marchionni. The mosaics, made between 1877 and 1883, artfully show how the craftsmen were aware of keeping traditions up to date; the Japanese stylisation of the two bunches of flowers, the post Macchiaioli (Florentine impressionist painting) style of the scene with the little girl in the garden and also the luxuriant taste of *Flora*'s personification, forerunner to the female prototype which was to have considerable success in the paintings and graphics of the *Belle Epoque*.

Flower stand

This work, like the others in this room and the last room, belongs to the final phase of artistic activity in the Opificio when the Workshop's creations were destined to be sold to the public to finance and maintain the old Medici institution. However, the ambition and quality of the work remained at the level of the grand traditions of the past, as seen in this monumental flower stand. The lower part, even with valuable Siberian lapis lazuli in the base, seems more solemn than graceful, but the crown makes up for it by being a precious and seductive masterpiece, entirely covered

◀◀p. 47, no. 2

Panel with a large vase of flowers

This spectacular piece, finished in 1879, confirms the Opificio's obstinate pursuit of its vocation in spite of the little success achieved with the public. The people were scared away by the high costs involved in producing works as extravagant in their conception as they were refined in their finished effect. In the records of the time the large panel is in fact quoted as being a 'rectangular form to be used as a door or part of a large cabinet'. This description shows that the work was conceived for a piece of furniture of royal dimensions, a theory in line with the elegant composition and chromatic importance of the vase full of flowers. The vase stands on a pedestal surrounded by a 'window' like frame which creates a precious setting. The jewelled effect of the frame, created by the vibrant colour gradations of the petrified wood, is increased by the presence of false settings in gilded chalcedony. The settings hold crystal gems and 'buttons' of lapis lazuli

laid in a background of opalescent oriental chalcedony. Marchionni, the last and gifted *genius loci* of the Opificio's rich history, was the creator of the design for this piece. It is one of the last great works to come out of the Workshop which closed down after being magnificently active for over three centuries.

SOME OF THE MOST FRE-
QUENTLY USED STONES
FROM THE SAMPLES

Agate

This is a variety of chalcedony from the quartz family shown by the typical multi-coloured concentric or mottled layers. It has been used since antiquity and has a hard consistency. It can be found in different colours and in different parts of the world; the most common types are from Sicily and Goa (sanguine in colour), and also the sardonyx variety which is translucent and irides-cent. The use of the *Sabina* variety is more recent and can be seen in mosaics.

Alabaster

This is a soft stone with a compact and opales-cent appearance; the chalky variety was one of the most frequently used stones in the Volterra area and the Etruscans were aware of its existence. The most resistant, cal-careous varieties are called: *fiorito (flowery) alabaster*, oriental in origin with various different appearances, and *cotognino alabas-*

ter, Egyptian in origin with characteristically wavy marks. The rar-est variety is called *ma-rine alabaster* and has an iridescent green colour with a red and bluish grain.

Basalt

This is a volcanic rock which is dark or black in colour.

Egyptian nephrite

This is a form of amphi-bole; a mineral made up of calcium, iron and magnesium. It can be opaque or translucent and can be found in different colours.

Granite

This is a volcanic stone mostly made up of quartz and used for sculptural work such as baths and sarcoph-agi. The most com-mon varieties are from Egypt and Elba.

Jasper

This is a common va-riety of quartz which is compact, opaque and resistant and was used in antiquity. It can be found naturally in different colours for example the *Barga* va-riety from the Garfag-nana region in Italy has white and pink markings while the *Corsica* variety has a green-blue colour. There are also varieties of jasper from Sicily and from Bohemia.

Lapis Lazuli

This is a precious stone with a characteristic blue colour. It contains specks of pyrite which give it a distinctive golden luminescence. In the 16th century the best stones came from Afghanistan in Persia. These were substituted at the end of the 17th century by stones from Siberia in Russia.

Limestone (*alberese*)

This is a calcareous stone with a soft consistency; it has different names depending on its natural colours and appearance. It was appreciated for its creative markings and was easily found along the river Arno. The varieties include: *tiger Arno*, a pale yellow stone with brown markings; *lined Arno*, a stone with parallel wavy grey-brown lines and *pietra paesina*, a stone with fault lines which make it look like a countryside landscape. These were used both for inlay work and as backgrounds for oil painting.

Malachite

This is a material which originates from the alteration of minerals in copper. It has a characteristic blotchy green/dark green colour. Siberian malachite from Russia is very well known.

Marble

This is a calcareous metamorphic rock which is well suited to mosaic inlay work for ornamental motifs and borders. The most well known varieties include: *antique black and white* from Aquitania and *antique green* from Tessaglia. Other varieties include: *Flemish paonazzetto* (made up of white marble and purple coloured cement), *Africa, Belgian black* and *Spanish brocatelle*.

Porphyry

This is a volcanic rock mostly made up of quartz with a very hard consistency and it is usually red in colour. One of the most well known varieties comes from Egypt.

Rock crystal

This is a variety of colourless transparent quartz which was mainly found in the Alps. The purple tinged variety is called *amethystine quartz* and was widely used in mosaics.

Silicified wood

This is an organic fossil which turns into a substance with the properties of a semiprecious stone through the process of silication.

Slate

This is a metamorphic rock which is supple to work with.

Translucent chalcedony

This is a variety of transparent quartz which was mainly used for mosaic inlays. It can be found naturally in various colours; the red variety is known as *corniola* and the brown variety is called *sardonyx*. The rarest variety is called *oriental* because of its origins in the East Indies.

Persian lapis lazuli

Persian lapis lazuli

Persian lapis lazuli

Persian lapis lazuli

Persian lapis lazuli

Siberian malachite

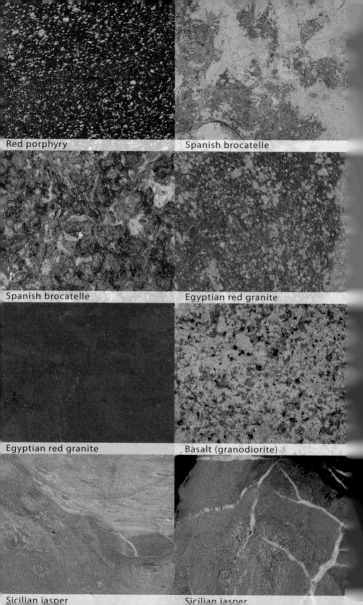

Red porphyry

Spanish brocatelle

Spanish brocatelle

Egyptian red granite

Egyptian red granite

Basalt (granodiorite)

Sicilian jasper

Sicilian jasper

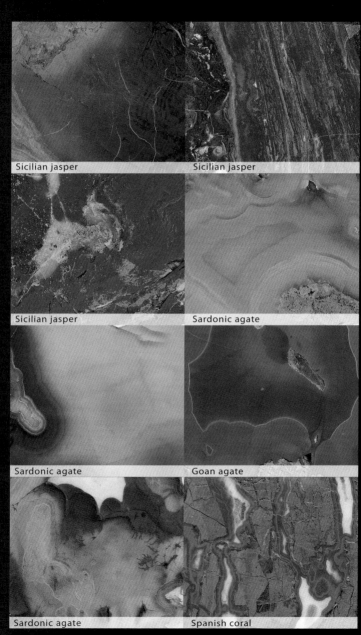

Sicilian jasper

Sicilian jasper

Sicilian jasper

Sardonic agate

Sardonic agate

Goan agate

Sardonic agate

Spanish coral

Commesso or Florentine mosaic

This type of mosaic derives from the *opus sectile* from Roman times and is made up of polychrome stone pieces. The stones are all cut according to well structured outlines and laid perfectly together to form a complete image. The perfect cut, the way the sections are joined together and the careful choice of the stones for their natural colour variations all contribute to the finished image's triumphal effect.

The mosaic's pictorial quality depends on the stones' colours but its value is increased further by the polishing of the stone surface.

Glyptics

The term glyptics has Greek origins and is used to identify the art of working semi-precious stones to carve cameos and to incise jewels. In the Medici workshops in the 16th century the term glyptics was mainly used for the carving of precious stone vases. It was later used

for polychrome mosaic sculptures made out of individually worked semi-precious stones; the stones were united to form work in relief or little statues in the round.

Stone on stone

This is an artistic genre which was especially popular in the 17th century. It was based on the union between the artist's imagination and nature's creativity. The painting's base was in fact a slab of stone whose natural mark-ings and colour varia-tions provided the back-ground for the subject; the paintings were done in oils. This genre was widely seen in Florence and the stone of choice was almost always the local limestone. Two varieties were used: the 'lined Arno' which evoked aquatic scenes, and the 'pietra paesina' which was perfect for creating rugged land-scapes.

Scagliola

This is a technique which involves gesso, colour and glue. In spite of the inferior materials the 'scagliola' was en-nobled by the way it im-itated precious marble surfaces. It was made using an inlay tech-nique similar to that of the stone mosaics which it sought to rep-licate. It was first used in Carpi at the begin-ning of the 17th century and acquired lasting and widespread popu-larity both for religious works and for furniture like table tops, cabinets and decorative framed scenes.

printed in April 2007
by Media Print-Livorno
for
s i l l a b e

www.sillabe.it
info@sillabe.it